SOUTHWEST BRANCH
ROCK ISLAND PUBLIC LIBRARY
9010 Ridgewood Road
Rock Island, IL 61201

Condition Noted. pg 11-12 taped

Counting Books

Beaches and Bicycles

A Summer Counting Book

by Rebecca Fjelland Davis

Reading Consultant: Jennifer Norford
Senior Consultant: Mid-continent for Research and Education

Capstone
press

Mankato, MN

A+ Books are published by Capstone Press,
151 Good Counsel Drive, P.O. Box 669, Mankato, Minnesota 56002.
www.capstonepress.com

© 2006 Capstone Press. All rights reserved.
No part of this publication may be reproduced in whole or in part, or stored in a retrieval
system, or transmitted in any form or by any means, electronic, mechanical, photocopying,
recording, or otherwise, without written permission of the publisher.
For information regarding permission, write to Capstone Press,
151 Good Counsel Drive, P.O. Box 669, Dept. R, Mankato, Minnesota 56002.
Printed in the United States of America

1 2 3 4 5 6 11 10 09 08 07 06

Library of Congress Cataloging-in-Publication Data
Davis, Rebecca Fjelland.
  Beaches and bicycles: a summer counting book / by Rebecca Fjelland Davis.
  p. cm.—(A+ books. Counting books)
  Includes bibliographical references and index.
  ISBN-13: 978-0-7368-5378-1 (hardcover)
  ISBN-10: 0-7368-5378-2 (hardcover)
  1. Counting—Juvenile literature. 2. Summer—Juvenile literature. I.
Title. II. Series.
QA113.D377 2006
513.2'11—dc22   2005019060

Credits
Jenny Marks, editor; Ted Williams, designer; Karon Dubke, photographer; Kelly Garvin,
    photo researcher

Photo Credits
Brand X Pictures, 18–19 (all), 23 (large flower, left)
Bruce Coleman Inc./Kim Taylor, 14 (all), 15 (top), 27 (butterflies)
Capstone Press, Karon Dubke, cover (all), 2–3 (all), 6–7, 10–11 (all), 12–13 (all), 16–17 (all), 20–21
    (all), 26 (ice pops, frogs), 28, 29 (all)
Comstock Images, 8–9 (all)
Corbis/Owaki-Kulla, 22–23 (smaller flowers, center), 26–27 (sunflowers); zefa/Laureen Morgane,
    24–25
Photodisc, 15 (bottom), 23 (2 large flowers, right)

Note to Parents, Teachers, and Librarians
Beaches and Bicycles uses color photographs and a rhyming nonfiction format to introduce children
to various signs of the summer season while building mastery of basic counting skills. It is designed
to be read aloud to a pre-reader or to be read independently by an early reader. The images help
early readers and listeners understand the text and concepts discussed. The book encourages further
learning by the following sections: Facts about Summer, Words to Know, Read More, Internet Sites,
and Index. Early readers may need assistance using these features.

The days are long and school is over.

The fields are full of sweet green clover.

Summer is the season for fun, fun, fun.

Let's count things under summer's sun.

One summer sun is a huge,
bright dot. Warm sun rays
make the days so hot.

Two round wheels, come, let's race! Summertime moves at such a fast pace.

3

Three red canoes.
As the days get hotter,
take a lazy trip through
cool lake water.

Four green frogs with big, round eyes look around for a meal of flies.

4

5

Five round beach balls,

colorful and fun.

Bounce them around

in the summer sun.

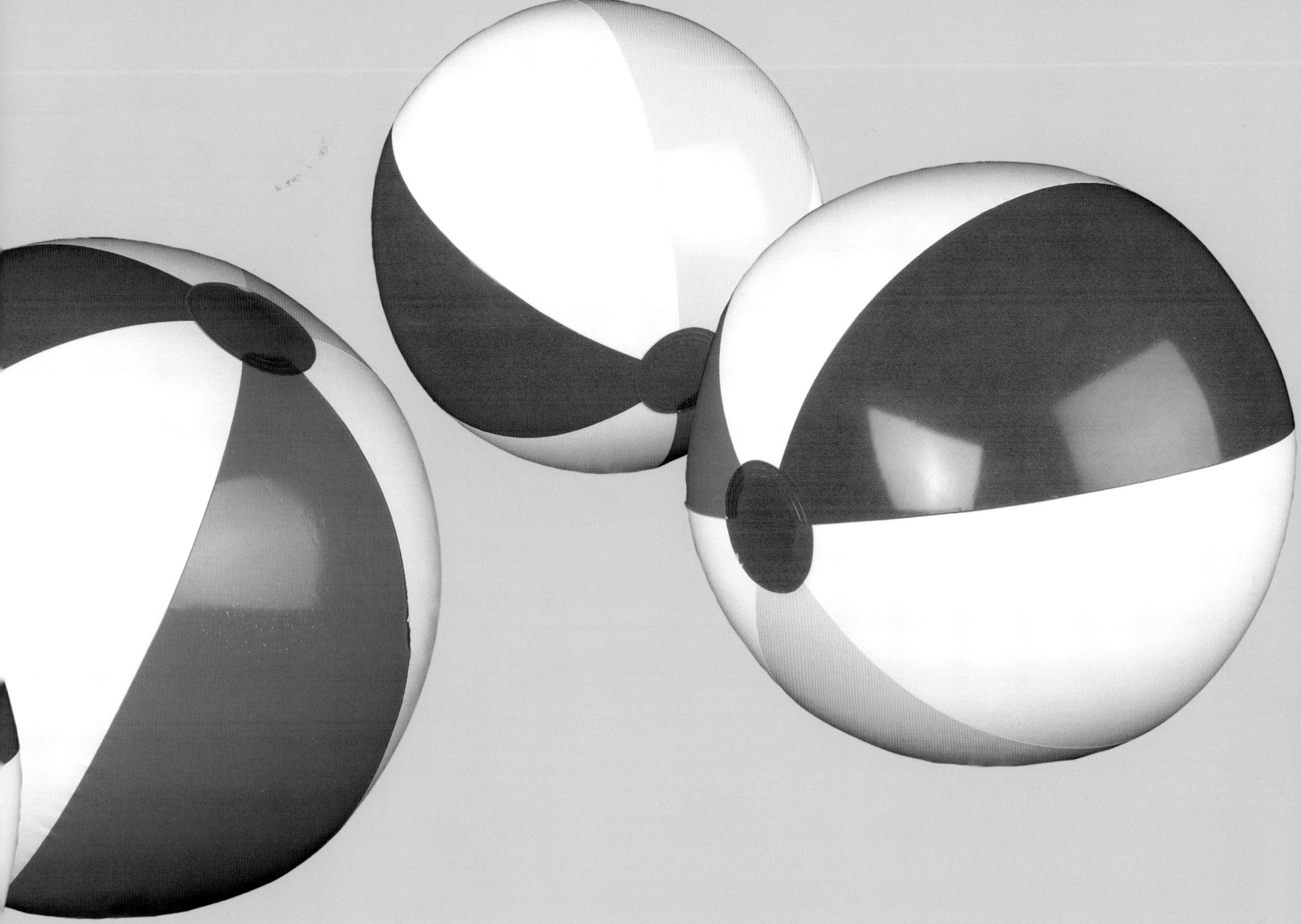

1
2
3
4
5
6
7
8
9
10

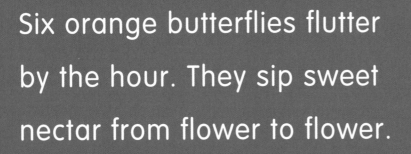

Six orange butterflies flutter by the hour. They sip sweet nectar from flower to flower.

6

15

7

Seven fruity ice pops
taste so sweet.

Just what you need
in the summer heat.

16

17

Eight tiny ants go marching in a row. Where there's a picnic, they seem to know.

9

Nine baseball gloves
for the game today.
Batter up! Come on,
it's time to play!

Ten yellow sunflowers all face the sun. When their petals start to fade, summer is done.

Summer's days are lazy, long, and hot. So find your way to a cool, wet spot.

How Many?

Ice pops

Frogs

Butterflies

Sunflowers

27

Facts about Summer

The sun is higher in the sky in the summer than it is in the winter.

In summer, the days are longer than the nights. In some places, like northern Alaska, the days are 24 hours long.

When it is summer in North America, it is winter in South America.

When a frog egg hatches, a tadpole comes out. A tadpole has no legs and looks like a little fish. Soon, legs sprout and the tadpole's tail shrinks away. The tadpole then becomes a frog.

Butterflies drink nectar from flowers.
Bumblebees and hummingbirds do too.

Butterflies have taste buds on their feet. They step
on flowers to know if the flowers taste good or not.

There are 20,000 types of ants in the world.
Some ants dig tunnels up to 15 feet long.

Sunflowers grow as tall as 15 feet. Some
have flowers 14 inches across.

Words to Know

batter (BAT-ur)—the player whose turn it is to bat in baseball

flutter (FLUHT-ur)—to wave or flap up and down; butterflies flutter their wings.

hatch (HACH)—to break out of an egg

nectar (NEK-tur)—a sweet liquid in flowers

petal (PET-uhl)—one of the colored outer parts of a flower

ray (RAY)—a beam of light

season (SEE-zuhn)—one of the four parts of the year; autumn, winter, spring, and summer are seasons.

taste bud (TAYST BUD)—a small organ that can tell what things taste like

Read More

Branley, Franklyn Mansfield. *Sunshine Makes the Seasons.* Let's-Read-and-Find-Out Science. New York: HarperCollinsPublishers, 2005.

Cronin, Doreen. *Click, Clack, Splish, Splash: A Counting Adventure.* New York: Atheneum Books for Young Readers, 2006.

Maurer, Tracy Nelson. *A to Z of Summer.* A to Z. Vero Beach, Fla.: Rourke, 2003.

Parker, Victoria. *Summer.* Raintree Sprouts. Chicago: Raintree, 2005.

Internet Sites

FactHound offers a safe, fun way to find Internet sites related to this book. All of the sites on FactHound have been researched by our staff.

Here's how:
1) Visit *www.facthound.com*
2) Type in this special code **0736853782** for age-appropriate sites. Or enter a search word related to this book for a more general search.
3) Click on the **"FETCH IT"** button.

FactHound will fetch the best sites for you!

Index